AF581674

The Greek-A-Pede Party

By Mary Louise Kelly
Illustrated by Jenn Sargent

ISBN: 978-3-200-10161-6

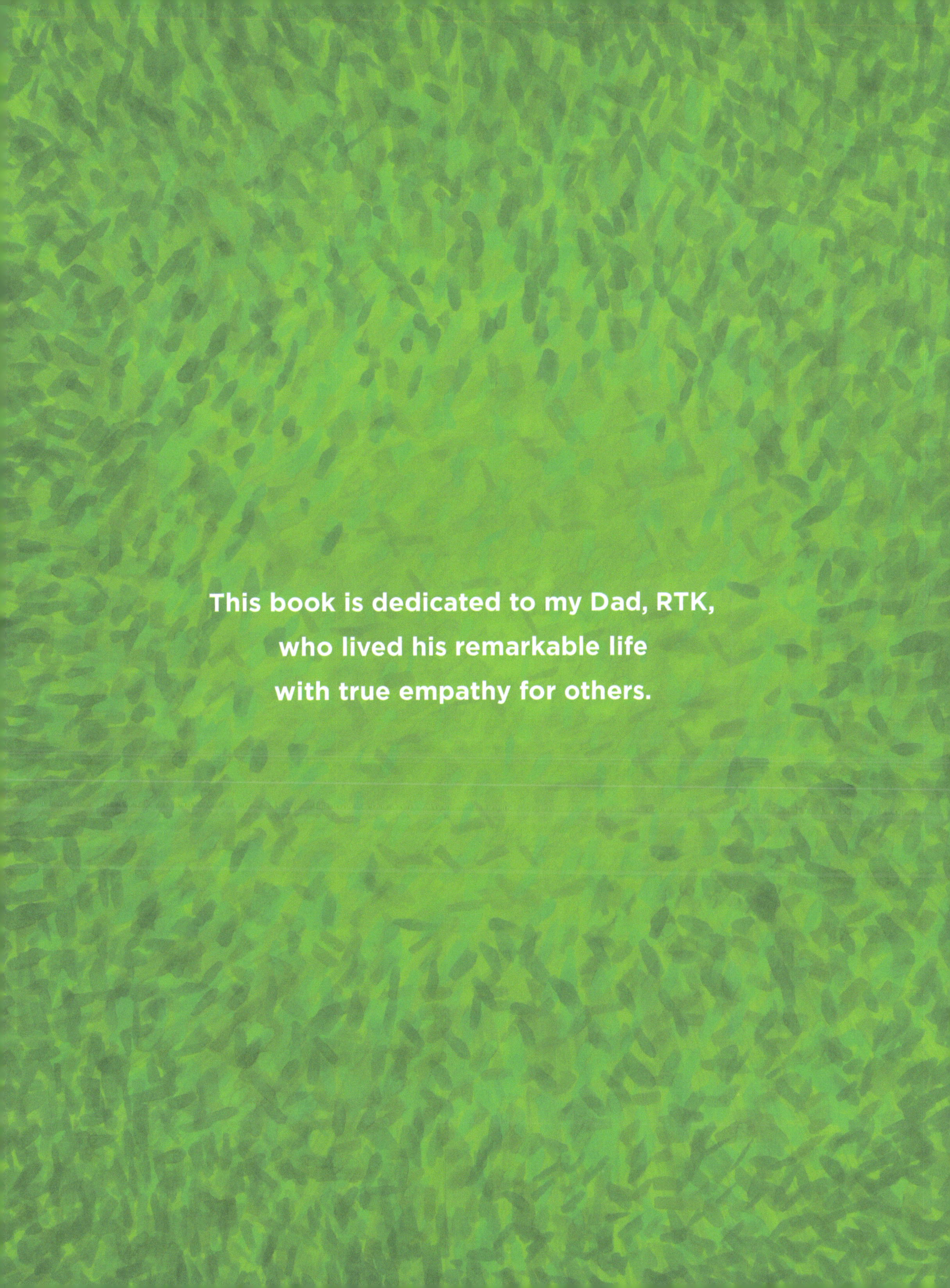

This book is dedicated to my Dad, RTK,
who lived his remarkable life
with true empathy for others.

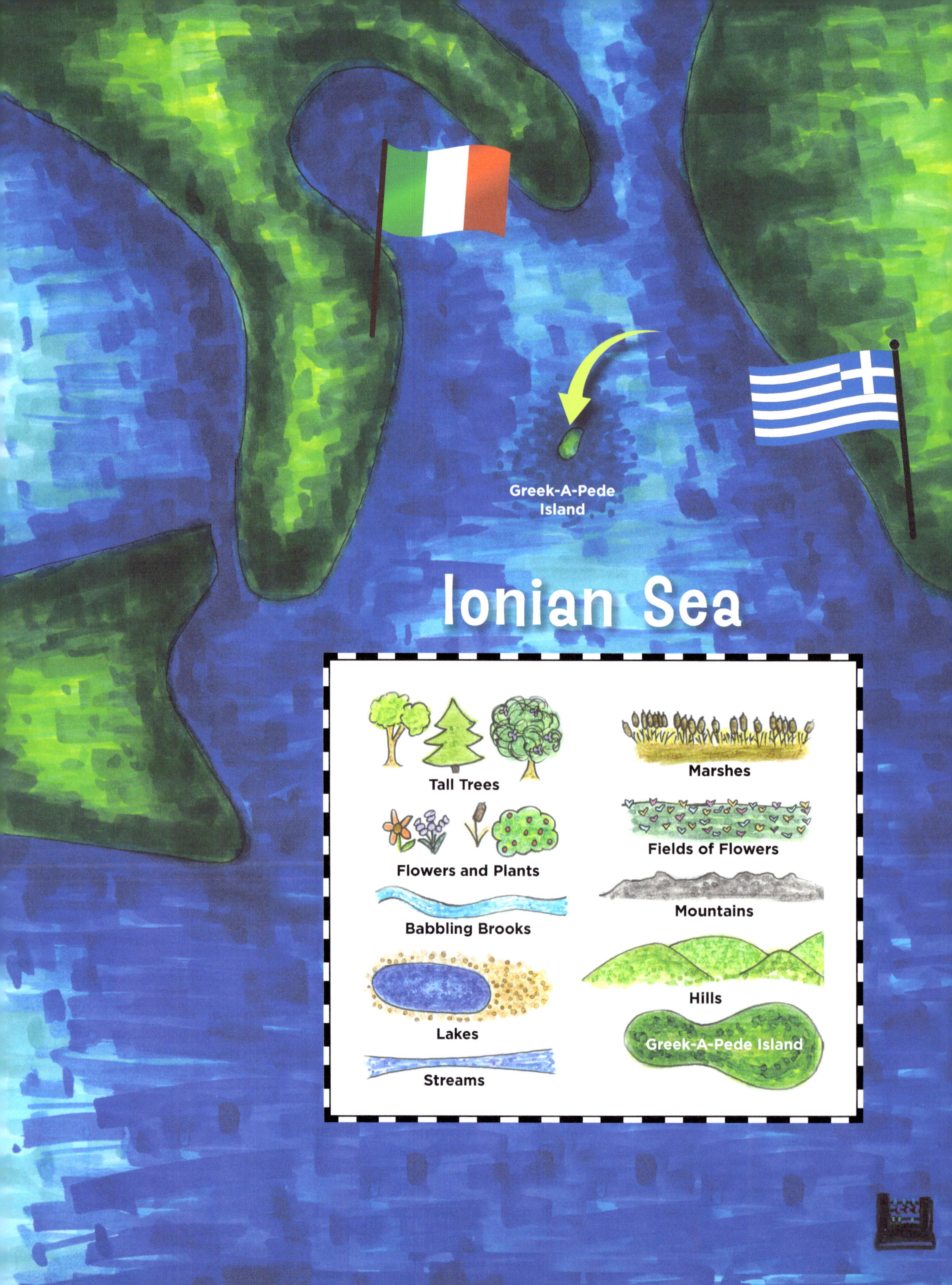
Greek-A-Pede
Island
Ionian Sea
Tall Trees
Marshes
Fields of Flowers
Flowers and Plants
Mountains
Babbling Brooks
Hills
Lakes
Greek-A-Pede Island
Streams

In the Ionian Sea
between Italy and Greece lies
a very small island.
This beautiful island is lush
with tall trees, fields of flowers
and plants of every variety.
There are babbling brooks, lakes,
streams, marshes, meadows,
mountains and hills.

The only known inhabitants of the island are thousands of tiny colorful creatures known as

Greek-a-pedes.

Every 10 years the
Greek-a-pedes unite for a
fantastically, joyful party.
It is a full day and
night of music and dancing,
food and drink,
singing and laughter,
games and entertainment.

Welcome to the
Planning Committee

The Party Planning Committee
works together for
many months to ensure
the success of the
Event of the Decade.
There are 10 members
of the planning committee
who represent the 10 tribes
who live on their
extraordinary island.

Dexter is a Decapede.
His body has 10 feet.
Deca means 10 in Latin.
Pede means feet in Greek.

—

Nora is a Novapede.
Her body has 9 feet.
Nova means 9 in Latin,
Pede means feet in Greek.

—

Oscar is an Octopede.
His body has 8 feet.
Octo means 8 in Latin.
Pede means feet in Greek.

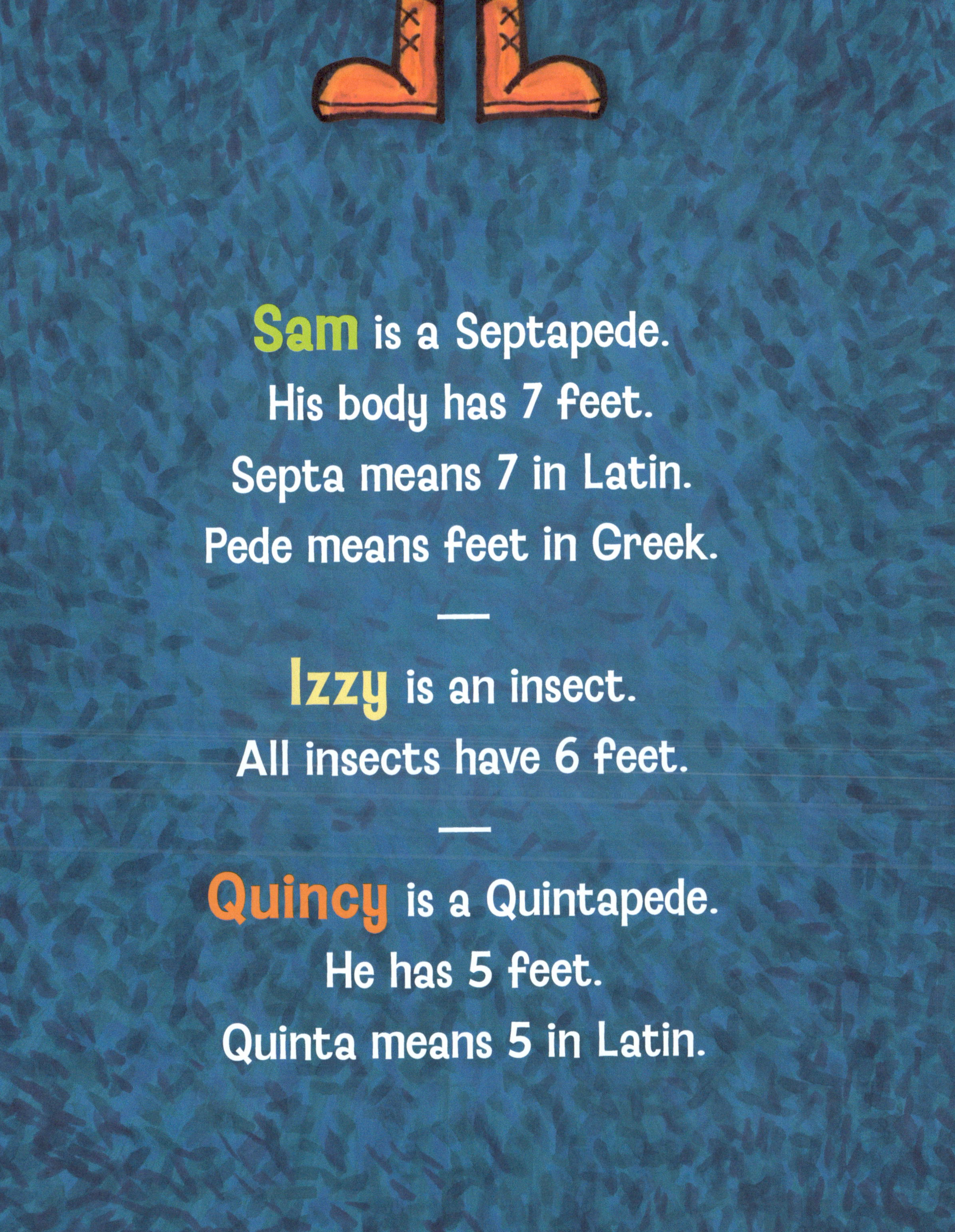

Sam is a Septapede.
His body has 7 feet.
Septa means 7 in Latin.
Pede means feet in Greek.

—

Izzy is an insect.
All insects have 6 feet.

—

Quincy is a Quintapede.
He has 5 feet.
Quinta means 5 in Latin.

Quinn is a Quatrapede.

She has 4 feet.

Quatra means 4 in Latin.

—

Tim is a Tripede.

He has 3 feet.

Tri means 3 in Latin.

—

Douglas is a Duopede.

He has 2 feet.

Duo means 2 in Latin.

Uli is an Unapod.
She has 1 foot.
Una means 1 in Latin.
Pod means foot in Greek.

Welcome to the Party of the Decade
Food
Music
Friends

Everyone on the island is invited to
this wonderful celebration.

The Pedes love to laugh, sing, dance, run,
crawl, twirl, jump, climb and clap.

The Unapods would always attend.
They would eat and drink,
laugh and sing with everyone.
They love the music and would
hop to the beat.

Decorations
Food
Drinks
Music
Games
Entertainment

At the final meeting
of the Planning Committee
before the Big Party,
Nora, the Novapede had
an idea to propose.

"Let's give our fellow Unapods
a way to also run, skip, dance, jump,
twirl, crawl, climb and clap
like the rest of us."

"How would we do that?"
asked Dexter.

Nora answered,
"We could ask for volunteers
to give one of their feet
and we could attach it
to a Unapod who would like one."

Yikes!
It's okay.

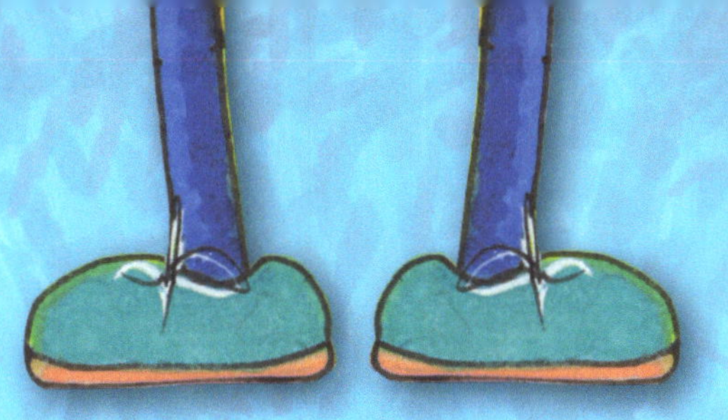

"Will it hurt to give up a foot?"
asked Oscar.

Nora replied,
"It would hurt a little bit for 1 second.
But if you look at the joy
on the face of the Unapod
who will receive your foot
you will also feel their joy in your heart.
And that is a wonderful feeling."

"How would we
attach a foot?" asked Uli.

"We could tape it," said Sam.
"We could tie it," said Izzy.
"We could sew it," said Quincy.
"We could knit it," said Quinn.
"We could pin it," said Tim.

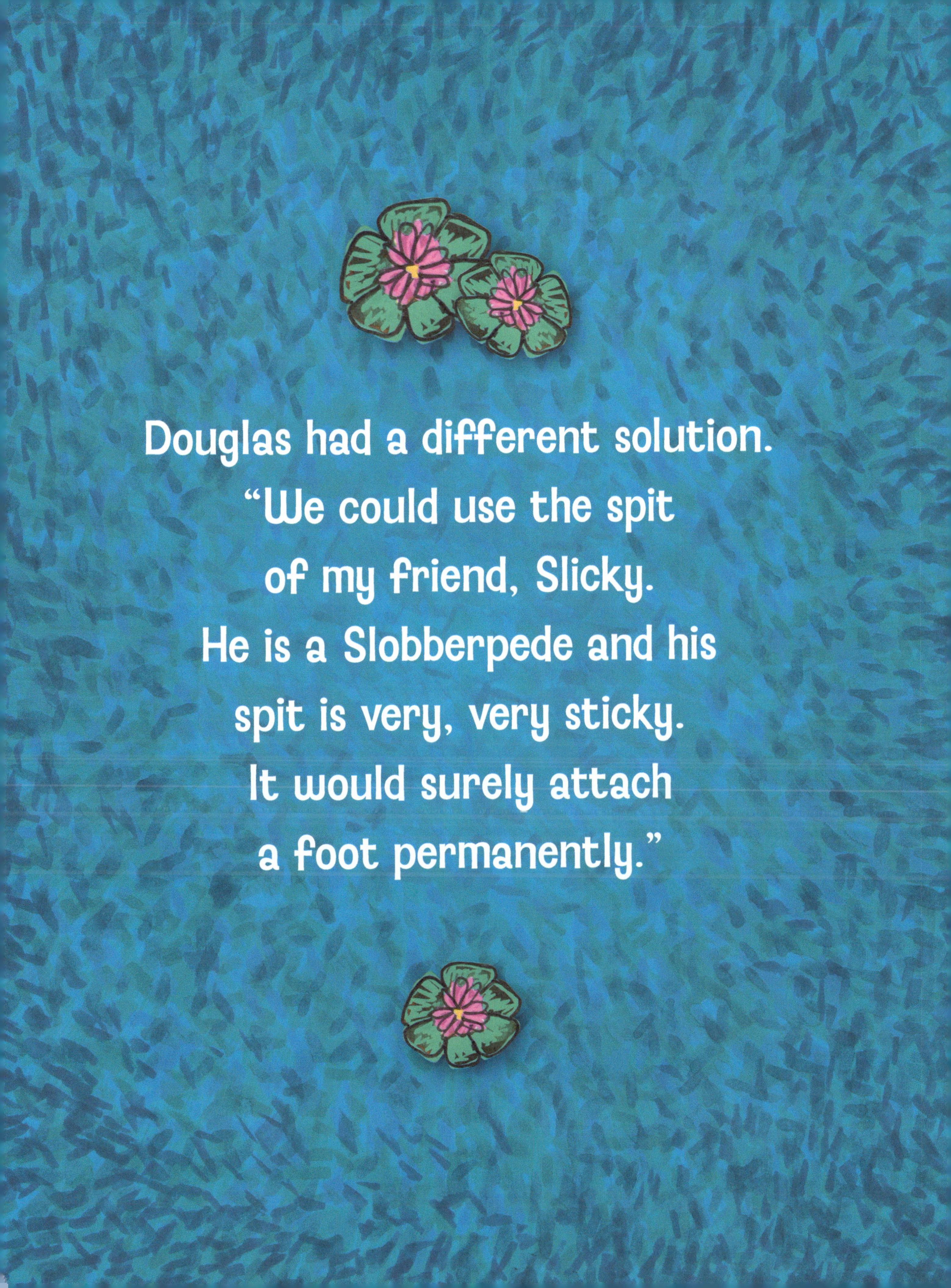

Douglas had a different solution.
"We could use the spit
of my friend, Slicky.
He is a Slobberpede and his
spit is very, very sticky.
It would surely attach
a foot permanently."

The day of the
Event of the Decade
finally arrived.
The Planning Committee
made a huge sign.

If you have a spare
And you care
Kindly share.

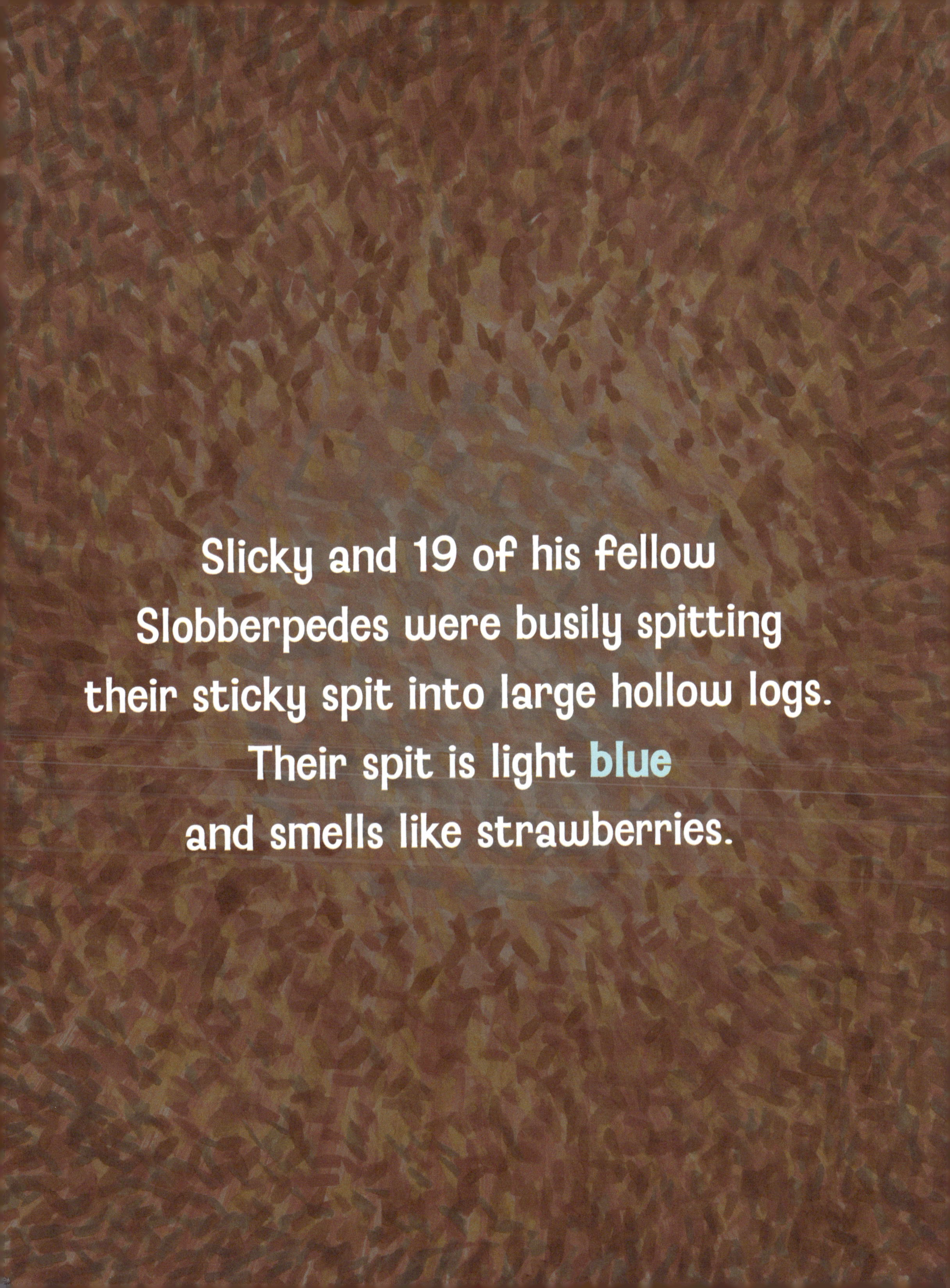

Slicky and 19 of his fellow
Slobberpedes were busily spitting
their sticky spit into large hollow logs.
Their spit is light blue
and smells like strawberries.

That night, more than
10,000 Unapods became Duopedes.

Hundreds of Decapedes became Novapedes.

Hundreds of Novapedes became Octopedes.

Hundreds of Octopedes became Septapedes.

Hundreds of Septapedes became Insects.

Hundreds of Insects became Quintapedes.

Hundreds of Quintapedes became Quatrapedes.

Hundreds of Quatrapedes became Tripedes.

Hundreds of Tripedes became Duopedes.

All the Duopedes remained Duopedes.

Although they did care,

they did not have a spare.

Each of the Unapods who became Duopedes

were very, very grateful for their new foot.

They practiced walking, running, jumping,

crawling, twirling, climbing, dancing

and clapping with their new feet.

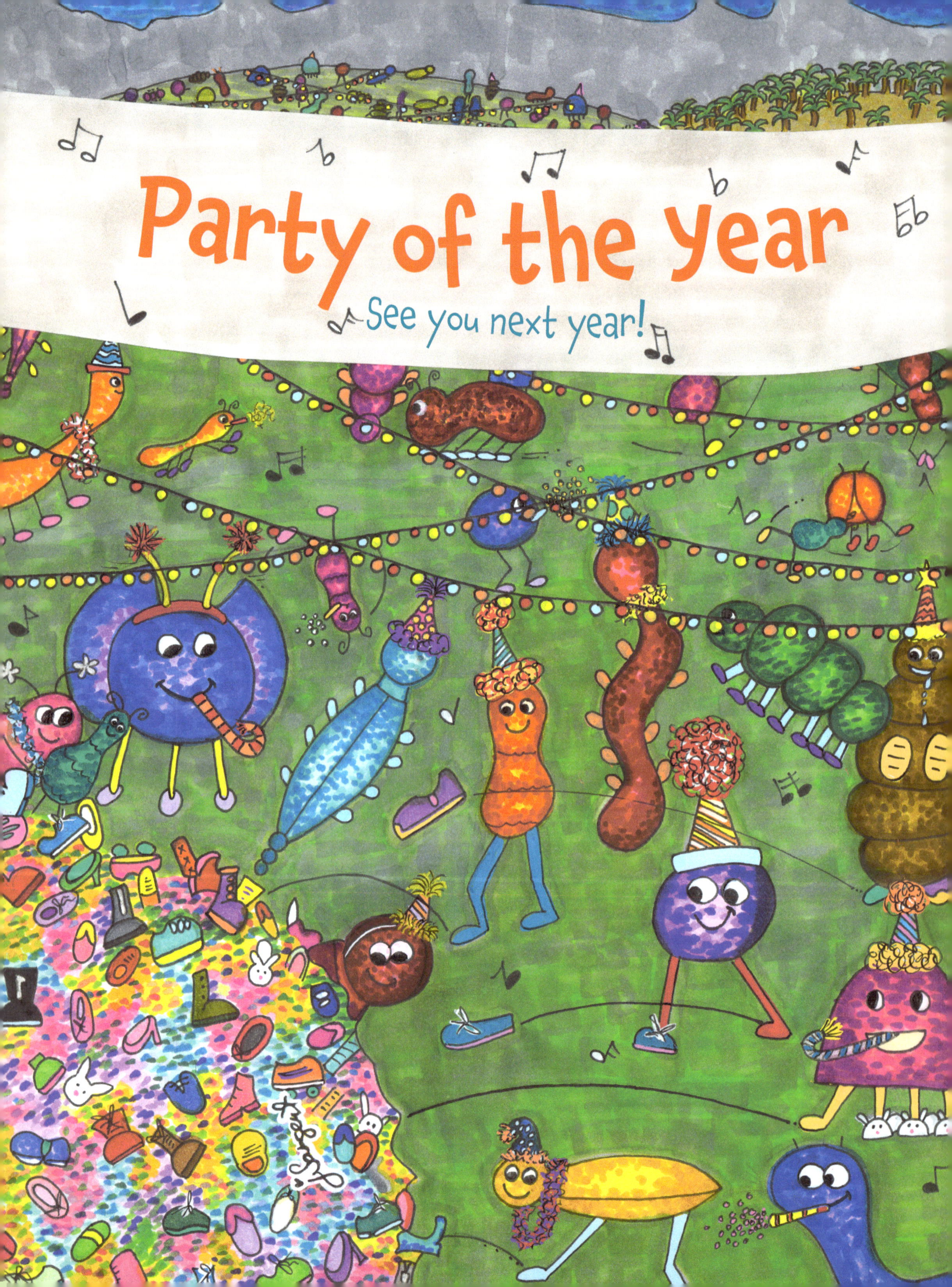
Party of the year
See you next year!

It was truly a party to remember!

“Ten years is a long time to wait for the next party,” said Uli.

The Planning Committee unanimously agreed. They decreed that instead of having this party every decade they will begin to plan for next year and make it an Annual Event!

Search and Find Hidden Objects

Search the book from cover to cover to find all of these hidden objects.

 **Abacus**

 **Binoculars**

 **Bicycle**

 **Basket**

 **Calendar**

 **Domino**

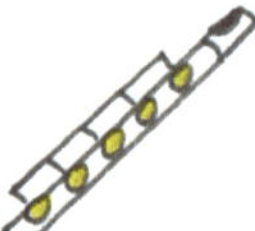 **Flute**

 **Flag**

 **Flame**

 **Goblet**

 **Letter**

 **Mallet**

 **Quilt**

 **Rope**

 **Ruby**

 **Star**

 **Scale**

 **Sword**

 **Signature**

 **Wheel**

 **Hook**

About the Author and Illustrator

Mary Louise Kelly, Author

Mary Louise was born and raised in beautiful Northeastern, Pennsylvania. Having earned her degree in Elementary Education with a minor in Exceptional Children she went on to earn her Masters Degree in Early Childhood Education. She was an Elementary teacher for more than 40 years. Her love of children's books as a learning tool has inspired The Greek-A-Pede Party, her third book. Her other teaching skills included working as a certified professional ski instructor as well as a volleyball instructor and coach at the university level. She loves traveling the world and has a passion for playing golf. She resides in "The Most Livable City In The World," Vienna, Austria.

Jenn Sargent, Illustrator

Jenn was born an Artist with the generous gift of growing up on the inspirational shores of the great Lake Michigan. Art school and all the rich experiences that come with it was the natural path for her. She earned a Bachelor of Arts degree from Purdue University with a double major in Art Education and Visual Communication Design. She minored in Fine Arts with an emphasis on painting. Jenn has always focused her time and effort discovering ways creativity and art can support and complement her communities.

Currently living in South Bend, Indiana with her husband and son Jenn enjoys working to bring colorful life to the adorable, kind and educational stories of Mary Louise Kelly. When she is not pushing colors, Jenn focuses on supporting and inspiring a rich public school experience for her son and their community. She continues to use art, energy, love and ideas to make a positive and lasting impact on those around her. "Art isn't something I do ... it's everything I am."